WEDGWOOD
MADE IN ENGLAND

DESIGNED BY
RAVILIOUS.

RAVILIOUS

The Complete Wedgwood Designs of Eric Ravilious

& WEDGWOOD

Richard Dennis

ACKNOWLEDGEMENTS

The publisher is indebted to all those who have contrib-
uted to the making of this book. Particular mention
must be made of Maureen Batkin and Robert Harling
for allowing their contributions to be reprinted. Grateful
thanks are also due to: the three Ravilious children —
John, James and Anne; Sharon Gater of the Wedgwood
Museum at Barlaston; Patricia Andrews and Brenda
Mason of the Towner Art Gallery, Eastbourne; the late
Edward Bawden; Helen Dore; Laura Russell; Judith
Turner; Barry and Saria Viney. The publisher would
also like to thank those who have given permission
for designs and photographs to be reproduced: The
Ravilious Family; Towner Art Gallery, Eastbourne; The
Trustees of the Victoria and Albert Museum, London;
The Trustees of the Wedgwood Museum, Barlaston.

First published in 1986
in a limited edition of 750 copies by Dalrymple Press
This edition published in 1995 and 2006 by Richard Dennis
The Old Chapel · Shepton Beauchamp
Somerset TA19 0LE
© Robert Dalrymple & Richard Dennis
All rights reserved

ISBN 0 903685 38 8

Production by Wendy Wort
Print & reproduction by Flaydemouse, Yeovil
British Library Cataloguing-in-Publication Data:
A catalogue record for this book is available
from the British Library

Contents

Eric Ravilious: A Memoir

Robert Harling

THE NAME RAVILIOUS is probably of Huguenot derivation, possibly Flemish, but the particular bearer of the name, the subject of this monograph, was as English as Palmerston. Indeed, no Hollywood casting director could have bettered the qualifications of Eric Ravilious to personify Pevsner's quizzical theory concerning the Englishness of English Art – and, presumably, artists.

For one thing, Ravilious looked the part. He could never have been mistaken for an artist from another land. At first meeting, I thought he looked more the cricketer he occasionally was than the artist he always was: tall, slim, modest, bonily handsome, mildly otherworldly, but quick to laughter, and with much of an undergraduate's carefreedom in manner and dress. This Englishness was doubly underlined by his wife, Tirzah, daughter of a retired sapper Colonel, petite, pretty, fey, carefree, and, incidentally, one of the most neglected and underestimated artists of her time. *

* The most endearing and enduring portraits of this fateful pair are to be found in Helen Binyon's book, *Eric Ravilious*, published by the Lutterworth Press in 1983.

Eric Ravilious by Phyllis Dodd, 1929
oil on canvas, $13\frac{3}{4} \times 11\frac{1}{2}$ in.
Ravilious family

The Ravilious achievement would have confirmed the accuracy of the casting. The engravings and watercolours (that most English of the arts) are as quirky, curious and indigenous as *Alice in Wonderland* or 'Greensleeves'; his visual passions clear to see: Boat Race Day, the bland downs of Sussex, the bleak hills of Wales, superannuated railway engines; vintage vans and the vagaries of village life. Husband and wife shared these interests, aided and abetted by the closest friend of their brief lives, Edward Bawden.

For those with any pronounced interest in the graphic, and what are oddly known as the applied, arts, the loss of Ravilious prompts poignant yet pertinent speculation. Other artists of rare Englishness were also lost in the Second War: Rex Whistler, although not a war artist, was killed in Normandy; Thomas Hennell was captured and disappeared in Indonesia, and Albert Richards, virtually just out of art school, was also killed in Normandy. They, too, were artists and illustrators. They, too, delighted in the lyrical beauties of their native countryside and its mildly dotty inhabitants. Had they lived they would undoubtedly have become even more assured in the work they did so consummately well and by which they were known. Ravilious, however, was a different kind of artist. He was that rarity: an artist *and* also an outstanding decorative designer. Most designers are apt to turn, more or less exclusively, to the graphic arts or to industrial design; most decorators are apt to turn to interiors. Ravilious was at the very beginning of a career which promised exceptional – and, more to the point – unpredictable versatility in the fine, graphic and applied arts.

He perished at thirty-nine. He had already proved that he was a notable wood engraver, a talented lithographer, and, above all, a watercolourist of the highest order. As Richard Morphet of the Tate has written: '. . . as time passes, it becomes increasingly clear that his stature was greater than has often been admitted.'* That stature continues to grow. Quite early in his career, Ravilious had shown that he was a designer of wide-ranging interests, and later designed items as different as furniture and alphabets, wallpapers and, as this present monograph shows, ceramics or, more accurately, decorative themes uncommonly well suited to the production of quotidian china ware.

Personal charm as well as achievement aided his early recognition. He was supremely easy to get on with, wholly without affectation or conceit, yet possessed of an invincible confidence in his worth and work. He was a most relaxed artist to work with, thus subtly relaxing, delighting and reassuring his patrons or would-be patrons. I was witness to this especial ease of manner.

I had admired and bought his paintings from the moment I saw them in his first exhibition in that delightful gallery which Arnold Zwemmer opened as a round-the-corner adjunct in Litchfield Street to his internationally renowned bookshop in Charing Cross Road. I also bought another in the second exhibition, this time at Tooth's, but I first met him when we were both involved with London Transport.

Frank Pick, then head of London Transport, was a man of taste in the eighteenth-century tradition, concerned with every aspect of design – from stations to timetables – within the great

*Introduction to *Eric Ravilious* by Helen Binyon.

agglomeration he directed. Logically, but unusually, he had recruited an architect, one Christian Barman, as his aide in these manifold endeavours. At the time I was typographical consultant to London Transport, frequently in touch with Barman. He telephoned one afternoon to fix a meeting to discuss the typographical design of a series of booklets London Transport was proposing to publish which would be devoted to country walks within those areas of the Home Counties served by Green Line coaches. He had commissioned engravings from Ravilious for the covers of these paperbacks. These were promised for the meeting. I recall Barman's unabashed delight on seeing the proofs submitted by the artist; and the artist's reciprocal delight.

Barman passed the proofs to me with a triumphant flourish at the success of his hunch, and, in due course, partnered by the splendid Curwen *Fat Face* display type, the booklets, with their bold covers, made their appearance and continued to be used for several years.

Around the same time, I was asked to redesign the typographical format of *Wisden's Cricketer's Almanack*. In company with such publications as *Bradshaw's* railway timetable and earlier editions of *The Concise Oxford Dictionary*, I thought little needed to be done. A diminishing number of traditional publications seemed to have got their format right first time, however long ago. All I did was a modest tidying-up of a small number of typographical incongruities, although I notice that Alan Gibson, writing recently in the sporting pages of *The Times*, referred to these adjustments as 'a major revolution in presentation' for the *Almanack*. Anyway, I still think otherwise. Although a player of squash rather than cricket, I was far too hooked on the sturdy little compendium the way it was, to change its format dramatically. Nevertheless, recalling that Ravilious had a special enthusiasm for the game, I suggested to the then publishers, Whitaker's, that he should be commissioned to engrave a new design for the title-page. His engraving of mid-nineteenth-century batsman and wicket-keeper was immediately accepted and has been retained until the present day,

and remains an ideal graphic introduction to one of England's most durable publications. I thought the design epitomized the intuitive understanding Ravilious brought to commission from commercial patrons.

The engravings which I have mentioned were in the same context as the many engravings Ravilious had made by that time: similar to those which had made the Kynoch Press Diary and Note Book of 1933 so significant in making known the uniqueness of the artist's technique and viewpoint. Here were all those aspects of the England he knew and relished: villages, fireworks, conservatories, railways, dog-carts, farmyards, and so on. These scenes, first boldly commissioned by Herbert Simon of the Kynoch Press, were soon taken up for further exploration, most notably by Oliver Simon of the Curwen Press, Robert Wellington (for his Contemporary Lithographs project), Francis Meynell of the Nonesuch Press and Christopher Sandford of the Golden Cockerel Press.

That the themes of these engravings should be used in books and adapted for lithographs was understandable. But the notion of transferring these English scenes to cups and saucers, plates and bowls, required an especially bold and imaginative patron.

Happily, Victor Skellern, who had known Ravilious at the Royal College of Art, was, by the mid-thirties, Head of Design at Wedgwood, certainly the right man in the right place at the right time as far as this part of the Wedgwood story is concerned. He was able to enthuse the Wedgwoods and commission trial drawings from Ravilious. Some account of these transactions will be found in the catalogue in this monograph. The patronage proved indulgent and triumphant. The idiosyncratic viewpoint, technique and humour of the artist were ideally suited for transfer to ceramic surfaces, and, much to his surprise, Ravilious discovered that native craftsmen had an innate talent for the transfer of his designs to what were, for him, new surfaces.

The achievement was considerable, but the marketing of these fresh and delightful designs has scarcely reflected, during the ensuing decades, the enterprise and commercial courage of Josiah and Tom Wedgwood and the imaginative flair of Victor Skellern, half-a-century ago. Undoubtedly, the war blunted the opening thrusts of the selling programme and Wedgwood themselves seem to have been somewhat apprehensive or lethargic in their marketing policies, echoing, no doubt, the views of the *Pottery and Glass Trades Review* that Ravilious was 'ahead of his time' in these Wedgwood designs. Nothing, of course, is farther removed from reality. 'Ahead of its time' is one of those hallowed defensive ploys by marketing men when presented with any product of unusual imaginative quality. The designs were – and are! – made for the intelligent middle-class market. And now, as the Ravilious engravings and watercolours become increasingly sought after by collectors, would seem to be the right time for a fresh effort to be made to see that more of these delightful services with their attendant jugs, bowls and side-plates might again be seen in the stores. In many ways the thought that this valuable, irreplaceable and unique treasure-trove is there in Barlaston, virtually unexploited, is saddening. They are untouched by time, as modern as the hour, in company with all true works of art, however grand or modest, whether stained glass sacerdotal windows or Bewick engravings.

I conclude these notes with a sombre recollection of my last meeting with Ravilious, a week or so before his death. I had recently returned from Iceland and someone at the Admiralty, probably Robert Goodden, then working on naval camouflage projects, must have mentioned to Ravilious that I had been around. We met. He was to fly to Rejkavik within a day or so, to continue his work as an official war artist. To my surprise, he was in khaki, the uniform of a Captain of the Royal Marines. I had expected him to be in naval uniform. I had forgotten that official war artists, when attached to the Royal Navy, were invariably enrolled in the Royal Marines. Ravilious wore the uniform with a certain degree of insouciance. His carefree collar and way-ward tie would certainly have roused the spleen of any senior officer of that most spick and span of martial outfits.

We walked round Trafalgar Square and then lunched in the National Gallery, continuing to discuss Iceland, the strange lunar landscape, the pretty girls, the fairly haywire wartime nightlife within the endless daylight. I was mildly surprised to learn that he was proposing to spend his sojourn with the RAF, and pointed out that there was a great deal of nautical interest to be found in Rejkavik. I also begged him to seek out two naval officers – Lieutenants Benham and Thomas RNVR, I seem to recall – with whom I had become friendly during my own spell ashore in Iceland. No doubt as therapy from their duties for Naval Intelligence, both were steeped in the study of Icelandic legend and language. They would have proved congenial and exhilarating companions in that northern outpost. He promised to look them up. Years later, I saw that in a letter to Tirzah he had mentioned his intention of making his number with Lieutenant Benham.

Then, no more.

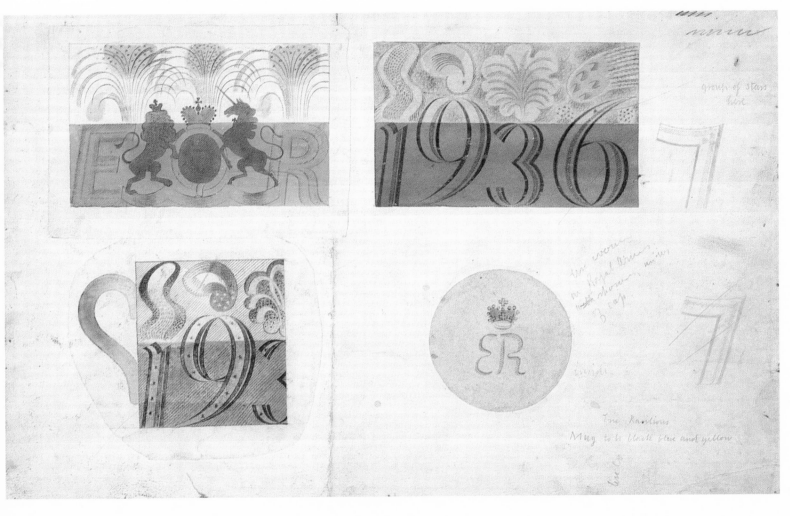

Coronation Mug 1936

Proposed Designs 1936

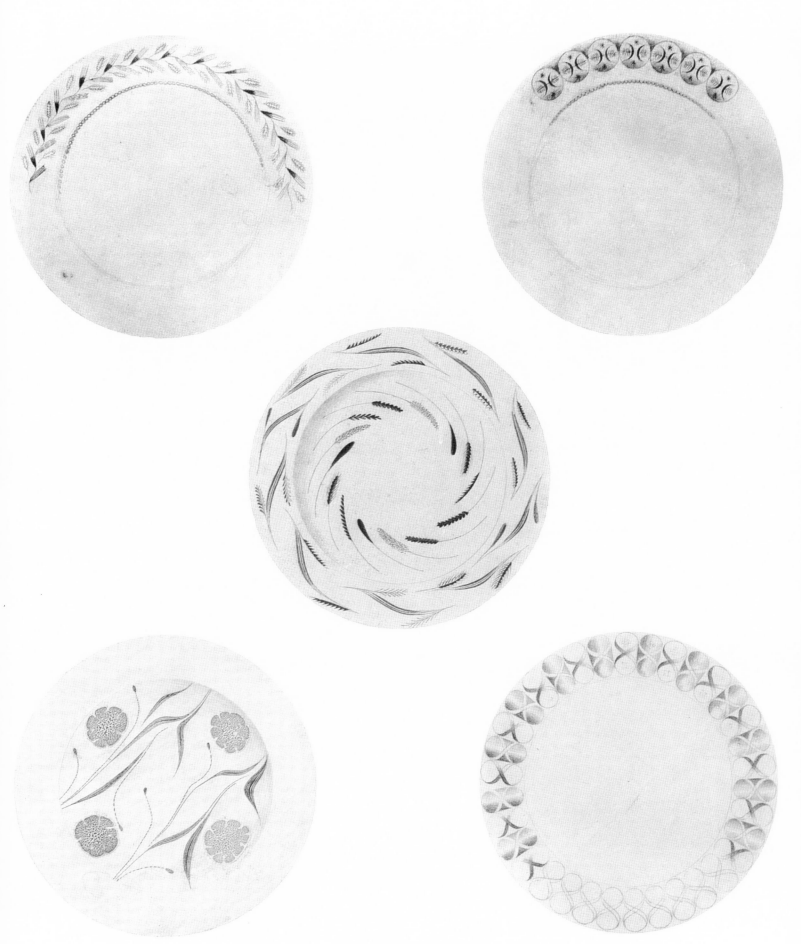

Proposed Designs 1936

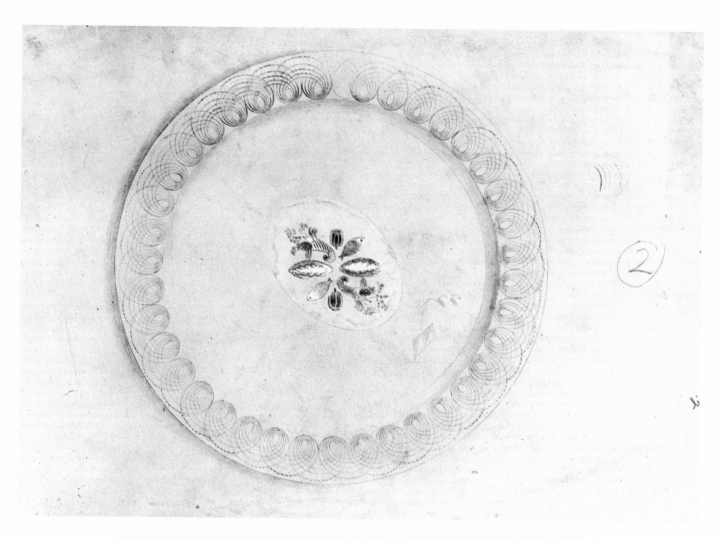

Persephone 1936

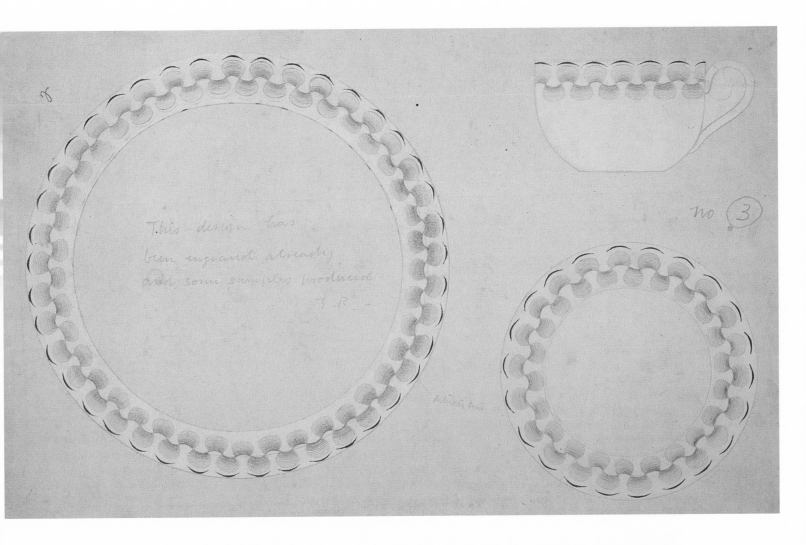

This design has
been engraved already
and some samples produced
J. R.

no ③

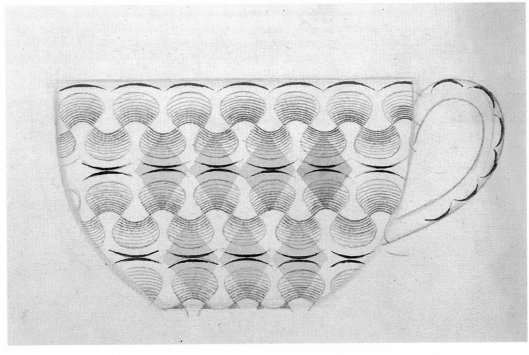

Troy 1936

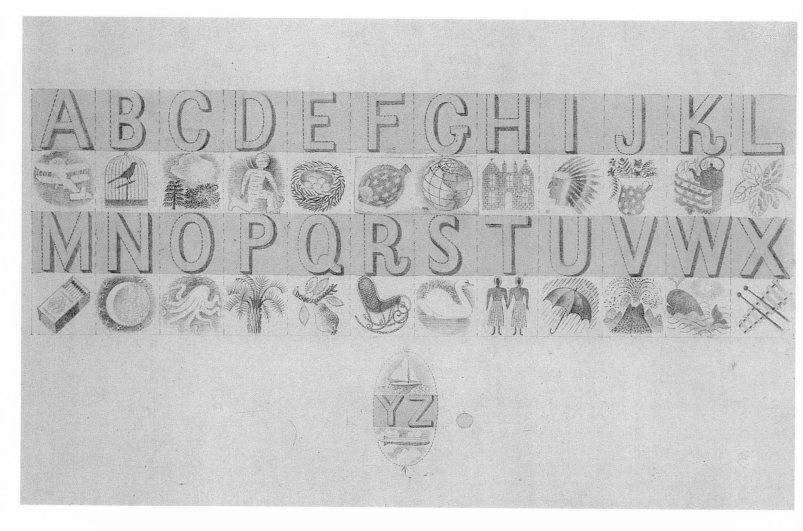

Alphabet 1937

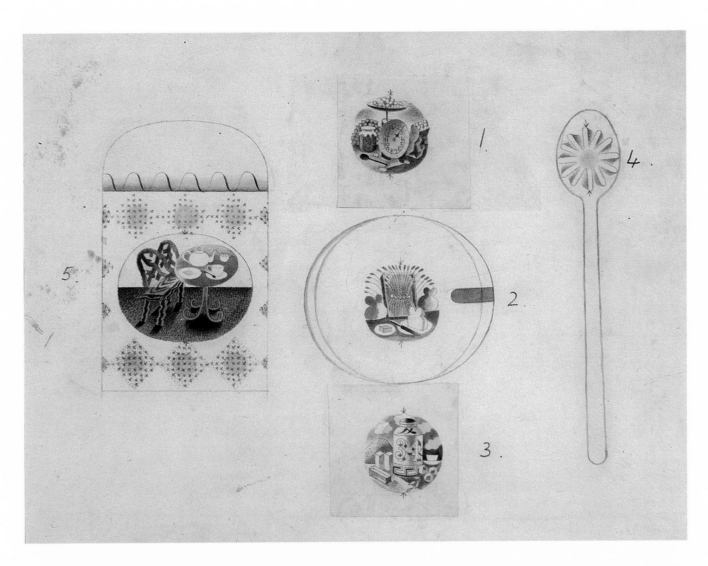

Afternoon Tea 1937

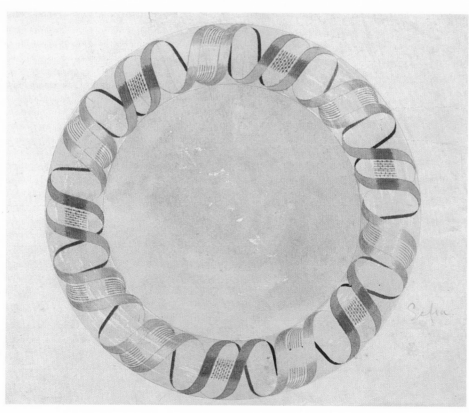

Proposed Designs 1937

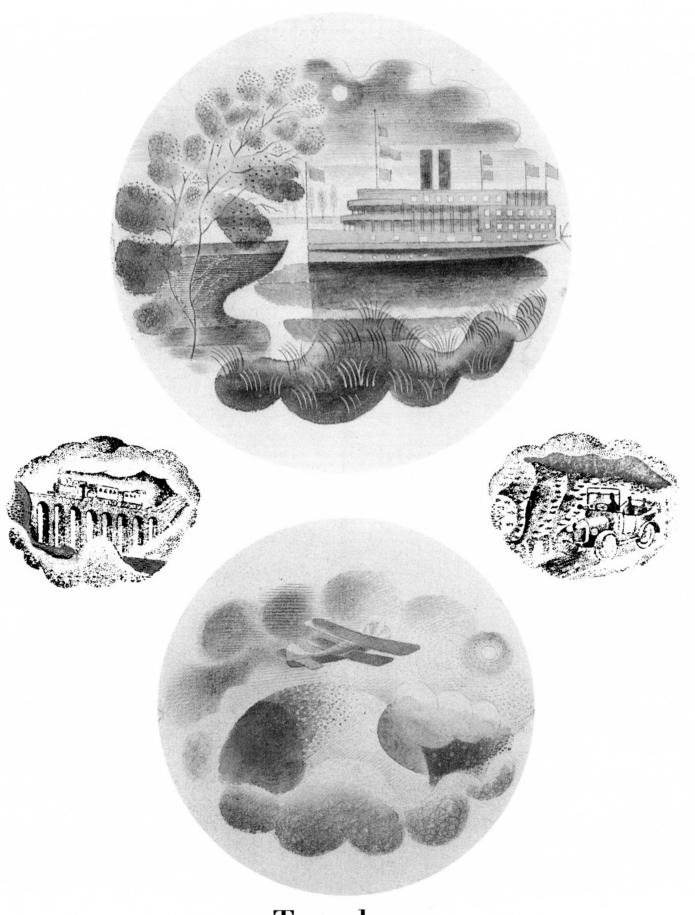

Travel 1938

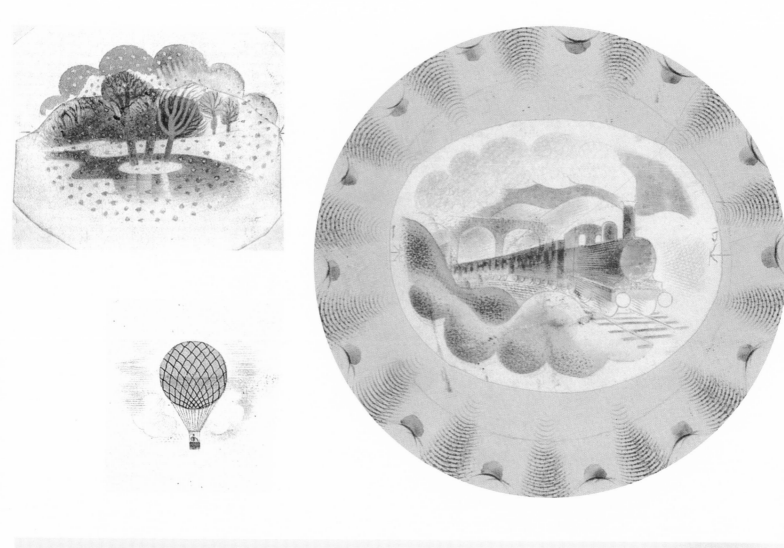

Travel 1938

Travel 1938

Boat Race Day   1938

Boat Race Day   1938

Garden 1938

Garden 1938

Garden 1938

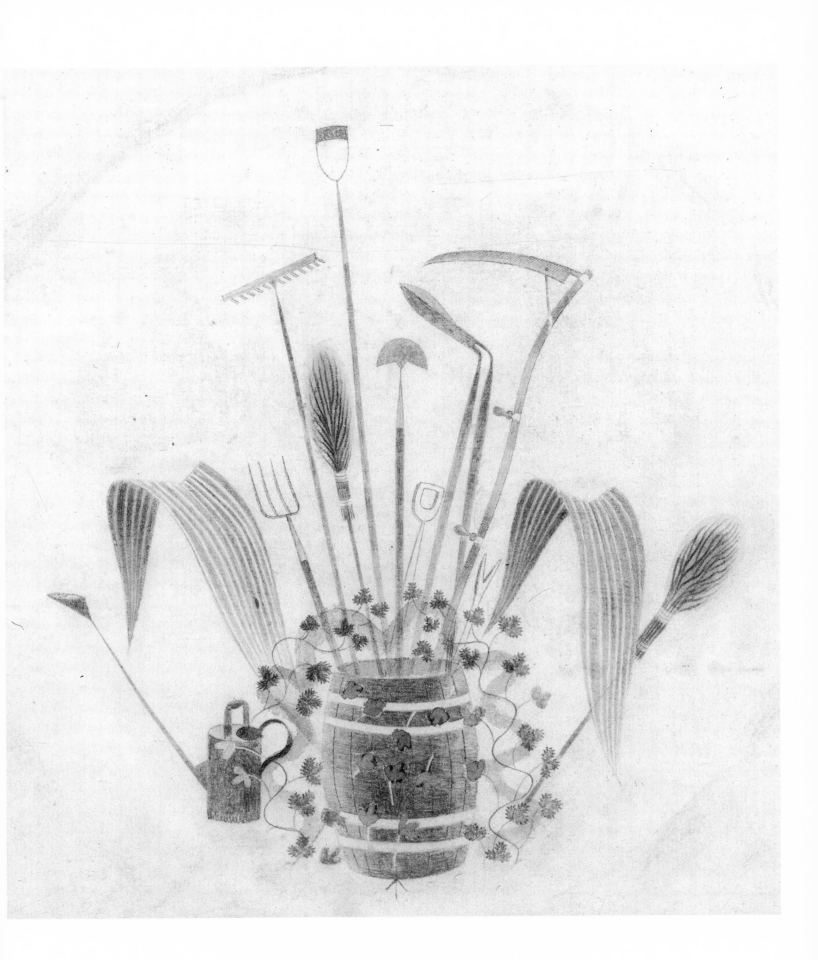

Garden Implements 1939

Garden Implements   1939

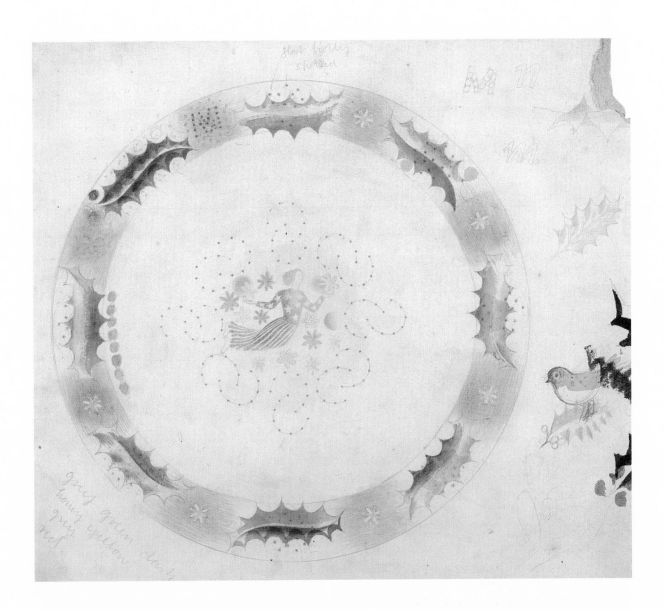

Noël 1939

Four Continents Bowl   1939

Four Continents Bowl 1939

London Underground Plate 1939

Barlaston Mug 1939

Proposed Designs 1937 & 1941

The Catalogue

Compiled by Maureen Batkin and Robert Dalrymple

The Process

Most of Eric Ravilious's designs for Wedgwood were intended for the traditional English method of transfer printing, introduced in the mid-eighteenth century, whereby patterns printed on tissue paper from specially inked copper plates were transferred to pottery and fired at a low temperature, the paper disappearing in the firing. Glazes were then applied and the pottery fired again.

Whereas the earlier Ravilious designs were engraved by hand directly on to the coppers by engravers at the factory working from pencil and wash drawings by the artist, the use of mechanical tints shows some of the later designs to have been photographically etched.

Two of the later designs were produced lithographically, the transfer being printed from plates drawn by the artist (see pp. 51 & 52).

Although Ravilious suggested the initial colouring of the design, it would appear that the many different colour ways manufactured were decided on at the factory, from the range of stock glazes, as production went ahead.

The Shapes

The designs were drawn to decorate Wedgwood's stock shapes. Many of these were traditional forms dating from the early years of the firm, others were new designs introduced by Victor Skellern and Norman Wilson in the early 1930s. Only one shape is thought to have been designed by Ravilious himself, the Teaset preserve jar (see p. 47); however, the shape used for the Barlaston and Coronation mugs was introduced specially for Ravilious's design.

Once a design was in production it was likely to decorate a great variety of different stock shapes. Unless the nature of the range was limited, as is the case with the commemorative mugs, 'Alphabet', 'Garden Implements' and 'Noël', it is impossible to be specific as to the full range of shapes decorated in any particular pattern. Nor has it proved possible to assess the quantities manufactured.

The Pattern Numbers

Every variation of a design which required hand-colouring, but not every shape on which it was used, was entered into the factory pattern books at the time of its introduction and allocated a coded number. The alphabetical code is as follows:

A   *Queen's Ware and other earthenware tablewares up to 1936*
C   *Queen's Ware and other earthenware 'fancies'*
K   *Underglaze decoration*
L   *Under– and onglaze decoration*
M   *Onglaze decoration*
T   *Queen's Ware and other earthenware tablewares from 1936*
W   *Bone china tablewares*

It must be noted that patterns were also produced without hand colouring, more particularly during the war years, and therefore not entered in the pattern books.

The Dates

In the absence of other information the dates given are the approximate date when the new design appears in the factory estimate and pattern books.

Coronation Mug 1936

page 17

Ravilious's first commission from Wedgwood was for a mug to commemorate the coronation of Edward VIII, expected to take place in 1937. Designed and produced in 1936, the mug was withdrawn on the King's abdication but not before Mrs Simpson had herself bought one from Dunbar Hay Ltd. The design was revised for the coronation of George VI and Queen Elizabeth in 1937, and again for Queen Elizabeth II in 1953. The original drawing for the mug was given by the artist to the Victoria and Albert Museum (E.292–1937).

In her memoir of Ravilious, Helen Binyon wrote:[1]

> All his life, fireworks were an important and special source of inspiration for Eric's work, and were made use of in many different ways . . . Eric had painted an elaborate watercolour of Bonfire Night,[2] as watched from the roof of their house in Stratford Road [Kensington]. He had found also that the white line of the engraving tools could be used most effectively for expressing the moving linear curves and starry patterns of fireworks, giving life and sparkle to many of the intricate designs that he made for publishers; these are quite distinctive and unlike the work of any other artist – a kind of abstract art.

PATTERN NUMBERS

Edward VIII Queen's Ware *introduced 1936*
CL 6203   printed sepia, enamelled turquoise band and egg yellow decoration

George VI and Queen Elizabeth Queen's Ware *introduced 1937*
CL 6203   as Edward VIII mug
CL 6225   printed sepia, enamelled marina green band and pale red decoration

Elizabeth II Queen's Ware *introduced 1952*
CL 6484   printed sepia, pink lustre band and lemon yellow decoration

TO COMMEMORATE
THE CORONATION
OF HIS MAJESTY
KING EDWARD VIII
—— 1937 ——
WEDGWOOD
MADE IN ENGLAND
DESIGNED BY
RAVILIOUS.

TO COMMEMORATE
THE CORONATION
OF THEIR MAJESTIES
KING GEORGE VI
QUEEN ELIZABETH
—— 1937 ——
WEDGWOOD
MADE IN ENGLAND.
DESIGNED BY
RAVILIOUS.

TO COMMEMORATE
THE CORONATION
OF HER MAJESTY
QUEEN ELIZABETH II
—— 1953 ——
WEDGWOOD
MADE IN ENGLAND.
FROM THE DESIGN BY
ERIC RAVILIOUS.

Wedgwood received the artist's first designs cautiously. In August 1936 Ravilious wrote from The Potteries:3

> This afternoon I'm going to the works again to have a look at the museum and make a few experiments. You will be sorry that the [Wedgwood] family think my beautiful designs above the heads of their public and that to begin with something should be done safer and more understandable. I argued about this most of the afternoon. The argument is whether to alter the present way of doing things in a hurry or to attempt it by degrees. I was all for a clean sweep and they want a method of slow percolation: it all means that I'd better think of some new designs – something if possible that suits all markets at once, so I must go back and see if I am clever enough to do this. The Coronation mug will be produced which is something; but you should see the one Laura Knight has designed, bloody beyond description. How she gets about that woman! The Wedgwoods say how bad the thing is but point out how big the sales will be. I wish her well but it seems a pity. Old Josiah's patterns are the most perfect pottery designs I've seen and they molder here because they haven't the wide appeal either – I believe we are the only designers the firm have had and it's a pity I can't raise his ghost to help along my argument. Dame L. K. must be giving him a turn just now.

Again, in October he wrote:4

> 'These pottery designs take so long to draw out. One is quite good so far. Wedgwood only like the fern plate with a border of balls [illustrated p. 18]. If he turns down the latest drawings I shall resign, but he won't this time . . .'

The other designs illustrated also date from this period and show Ravilious finding his feet. Two of the drawings incorporate wood engravings later to appear among his illustrations for *The Writings of Gilbert White of Selborne* published by the Nonesuch Press in 1937.

Persephone 1936
page 20

Designed and introduced in 1936 as 'Harvest Festival', the pattern is closely related to a drawing called 'Harvest Festival and Loaves',[5] made in the church at Castle Hedingham, Essex, where the Ravilious family lived. By 1938 the design was being advertised as 'Persephone', but when produced without hand colouring during the war years it was again named 'Harvest Festival'. The design was re-introduced in 1952 as 'Coronation Golden Persephone' and also adapted for use at the Coronation Banquet given by the Foreign Secretary in June 1953.

SHAPES   Various tablewares

PATTERN NUMBERS

Persephone Queen's Ware *introduced December 1936*
AL 9983   printed sepia, coloured and banded yellow
AL 9984   printed sepia, coloured and banded blue
TL 154   printed sepia, coloured and banded pink
TL 155   printed sepia, coloured and banded vine green

Coronation Golden Persephone 'Lincoln' bone china *introduced September 1952*

W 4133   printed gold, border and centre burnished
W 4134   as W 4133 but without centre cornucopia design
W 4153   as W 4133 but with ivory rim and gold edge verge line
W 4154   as W 4134 but with ivory rim and gold edge verge line

Queen Elizabeth II Coronation Banquet Service 'Lincoln' bone china *introduced June 1953*

as W 4133 but with the centre design replaced by the Royal Coat of Arms

Troy 1936
page 21

Designed in 1936 and introduced between January and March 1937 for the British Industries Fair. Although samples were produced as an alternative to 'Coronation Golden Persephone' in 1952, this pattern can never have been made in any quantity as examples are extremely rare. A drawing (illustrated on p. 21) survives for a variation of the design for the teacup but this was never manufactured. The pattern perhaps owes its name to the 'Grecian' shapes in which it was first made.

PATTERN NUMBERS

Troy 'Grecian' earthenware *introduced 1937*
TL 37   printed in sepia, painted scallops in red

Troy 'Lincoln' bone china *samples 1952*
W 4132   printed in gold

Victor Skellern, Head of Design at Wedgwood and known to Ravilious from his days at the Royal College of Art, recalled in the late 1950s:[6]

> . . . When he [Ravilious] first came, and being a very skilled wood engraver he was most anxious to have one engraver allocated to him with whom he could correspond and train to produce the style of engraving he had in mind. This was a bit of a problem, and might have caused a lot of trouble in the engraving shop, so I persuaded Ravilious to let us cut the first pattern and get his comments. I sent prints to him, and the reply was full of unbounding joy and enthusiasm – this was the engraver he wanted. I had found the right man who knew exactly what he wanted. When he next came to the factory and I had to admit that every one of the engravers – and there were ten of them – had each done a separate part of the engraving, he took this very well, and remarked 'I will never argue about the Wedgwood engraving any more, these chaps are without doubt the finest engravers I have ever met.'

Although this anecdote must refer to an earlier pattern, 'Alphabet' shows to good effect the complete sympathy between Ravilious and the craftsmen at Wedgwood.

SHAPES

Large mug, small mug, porringer, plate, double egg cup, jug, lamp base.

PATTERN NUMBERS

WEDGWOOD
MADE IN ENGLAND.
DESIGNED BY
RAVILIOUS.

Alphabet Nursery ware *introduced July 1937*
CL 6249   printed black, banded golden orange
CL 6260   printed black, banded pink
CL 6261   printed black, banded blue
CL 6262   printed black, banded vine green

Alphabet Nursery ware *revised c.1938*
In this version the plate has an additional colour band drawn under the rim.
CL 6328   printed black, banded pink
CL 6329   printed black, banded vine green
CL 6330   printed black, banded blue
CL 6331   printed black, banded golden orange

Samples of the pattern were also produced in black basalt glazed with gold lettering.

The main vignette of this pattern is adapted from a wood engraving commissioned by London Transport in 1936 to advertise Green Line Bus routes. In the drawing illustrated this appears on a preserve jar which, together with its spoon, are the only pottery shapes actually designed rather than decorated by Ravilious. The preserve jar was introduced six months in advance of the rest of the pattern. The design was advertised in 1939 as being available also in breakfast and coffee sets; the war prevented production of these. At first unnamed, later called 'Teaset', the design was finally named 'Afternoon Tea'.

SHAPES   Tea ware

PATTERN NUMBERS

Teaset Preserve Jar Queen's Ware *introduced 1937*
CL 6264   printed sepia, groundlaid green
CL 6265   printed brown, groundlaid green
CL 6266   printed sepia, enamelled yellow

Afternoon Tea 'Leigh' bone china *introduced February 1938*
W 3494   printed black, enamelled common yellow and emerald
green
W 3495   printed brown, groundlaid green
W 3496   printed black, groundlaid lemon yellow
W 3514   printed black, groundlaid green

Designed
by Eric
Ravilious

Proposed Designs 1937
page 24

Three of the wood-engraved patterns montaged to decorate the teacups are included in *The Wood Engravings of Eric Ravilious*, Lion and Unicorn Press, 1972; the other two patterns are previously unrecorded. These designs, and the plate design that appears beneath them, were never manufactured.

Travel 1938
pages 25–27

In December 1953 the *Pottery and Glass Trades Review* reported 'a new Ravilious pattern drawn before the War but now in production for the first time. Ahead of his time Ravilious designed for the generation to come and the public have just caught up with his Persephone – Travel may well prove a quicker winner.'

Two of the vignettes in the 'Travel' pattern are taken from earlier wood engravings by Ravilious: the aeroplane from his illustrations to *Fifty-four Conceits* by Martin Armstrong, 1933; the snow-storm from the *Kynoch Press Note Book* for 1933. The train scenes are adapted from an illustration to *The Hansom Cab and the Pigeons* by L. A. G. Strong, 1935. The other vignettes were designed in 1938, when all the coppers were engraved. A few trial pieces were made at this time, but the pattern was not put into general production.

SHAPES   Various tablewares

PATTERN NUMBER

Travel 'Windsor' grey fine earthenware *introduced September 1952*
TK 472   underglaze printed in black, enamelled in turquoise

Boat Race Day 1938
pages 28 & 29

In 1930 Eric and Tirzah Ravilious moved to Weltje Road, Hammersmith. The bay window of their flat looked out across Upper Mall to the Thames. This view provided not only inspiration for watercolour paintings but also the excuse for a party every Boat Race Day. Eight years later Ravilious drew on his memories of these celebrations in this design. A contemporary watercolour, 'Garden Flowers on Cottage Table'[7] shows the vase in its undecorated state. This indicates, as one might expect, that Ravilious would work up his designs with the blank ceramic body in front of him. The use of mechanical tints in the engraving shows this design to have been photographically transferred on to the coppers and etched. This may also explain why no original drawings have been traced. The pattern is reproduced on pp. 28 and 29 from the factory pattern book entries.

SHAPES   'Harvard' bowl (14 in diameter), 'Burslem' vase (10 in high)

PATTERN NUMBERS

Boat Race Day Queen's Ware *introduced 1938*
CL 6263   printed sepia, royal blue, blue, golden orange and pink
            decoration

The design was also adapted for 9 and 10 in diameter oval dishes with the addition of the Persephone border:
CL 6268   as CL 6263 with shaded blue band
CL 6269   as CL 6263 with golden orange border

In 1951 a promotional cup and saucer of 17 pint capacity was made in the design: the saucer is now in the Wedgwood Museum at Barlaston. In 1975 a 12 in diameter bowl was reissued in a limited edition of 200.

Garden 1938
pages 30–32

'Garden', the most elaborate of the designs (comprising a border, ten vignettes and many smaller details from these), appears in the Wedgwood estimate books between November 1938 and May 1939. 'Speaking for myself,' Tom Wedgwood wrote acknowledging the receipt of some drawings, 'I am delighted with them, particularly the Garden pattern; you must have put in a tremendous lot of work on these patterns since you were down here, and I do think you are to be congratulated on the result.'[8] As with the 'Troy' design, samples were produced in gold as an alternative to 'Coronation Golden Persephone'.

SHAPES   Various tablewares

PATTERN NUMBERS

Garden Queen's Ware *introduced 1939*

TL 259	printed sepia centre and border, enamelled golden orange (later changed to yellow)
TL 270	as TL 259 but enamelled blue
TL 275	as TL 259 but enamelled green
TL 284	printed sepia centre only, enamelled green and green line
TK 284	printed sepia centre only, colour and lined underglaze green for the Welwyn Parkway restaurant
TL 288	printed sepia centre only, coloured and lined golden orange

Garden Bone china *samples September 1952*

W 4141	printed gold centre and border, gold edge and verge line, print sanded and lines burnished

Garden Implements 1939
pages 33 & 34

The Wedgwood Museum at Barlaston has a collage annotated in Ravilious's hand showing one of the 'Garden' vignettes decorating a large 'Liverpool' jug. The difficulty of satisfactorily placing such an oval subject on this upright form probably prompted the artist to think again. The result was this related but independent design, 'Garden Implements': the motif being developed from the barrel on the plate on p. 32.

SHAPES   Lemonade set: 'Liverpool' jug and beakers

PATTERN NUMBERS

Garden Implements Queen's Ware *introduced 1939*

CL 6321	printed sepia, painted ivy green and lined black
CL 6322	printed sepia, painted yellow and lined black
CL 6363	printed sepia, painted purple and pink lustre and lined black

Noël 1939
page 35

'The Christmas pudding service is a very nice idea,' Ravilious wrote to Cecilia Lady Sempill in October 1938, 'and I shall remember it for next year. Did you know that I am going to experiment with lithography for decorating pots – I look forward to the change.'9 'Noël', although never manufactured, was to be the first of these experiments.

In 1936 Ravilious had drawn 'Newhaven Harbour: Homage to Seurat' for Robert Wellington and John Piper's Contemporary Lithographs series. The next year, fired by enthusiasm for the process, he drew twenty-four lithographs for *High Street*, published in 1938 by Country Life Books, with a short text by J. M. Richards. Both projects had been printed by the Curwen Press: 'under Curwen's tuition Ravilious had absorbed, with tremendous speed, not only the basic drawing techniques of lithography, but also the tremendous possibilities of a limited colour range when transparent colours are used'.10 The success of *High Street* led Ravilious to use these new-found skills in his designs for Wedgwood.

He wrote again to Lady Sempill in November 1939, 'By the way, Wedgwoods have sent at last completed samples of the Christmas pudding set, and have made a very good job of it . . . but not for this Christmas alas.'11 These samples were shown that year at the Arts and Crafts Exhibition in the United States and Canada (and are now in the Victoria and Albert Museum, E.309–1961), but the War brought production plans to a halt.

As Ravilious drew directly on to the lithographic plates, no finished drawing for the design exists: a working sketch is shown on p. 35. Although the design would have been allocated a pattern number, it has not been traced.

SHAPES 11 in plate, 8 in plate, soup dish, and sauce boat

Four Continents Bowl 1939
pages 36 & 37

At the 1939 New York World's Fair the Tate Gallery exhibited three watercolour paintings by Ravilious. In addition he engraved the cover of the brochure for the British Pavilion and designed a series of decorative symbols, engraved on copper and inlaid with enamel, for a great map illustrating the maritime commerce of Britain. The original drawings for these symbols decorate this bowl which Ravilious suggested to Wedgwood, but which was never produced. The drawing was included in the artist's memorial exhibition, 1948–9, entitled 'The Four Continents': this is something of a misnomer as scenes from all six are shown.

London Underground Plate 1939
page 38

London Transport's New Works Programme of 1935–40 planned the ambitious extension of the Northern and Bakerloo lines northwards, and the Central line both east and westwards. Although well advanced by the outbreak of war, the project had to be abandoned and was only partly realized in the post-war years. Thus the commemorative plate designed by Ravilious was never produced. The three heraldic devices show the county badges of Essex, Hertfordshire and Middlesex.

The plate would have been one of the last commissions of Frank Pick, chief executive of the London Passenger Transport Board. Pick, who retired in 1940 and died the next year, had worked for the Underground since 1906. Throughout his career his over-riding passion was for architecture and design, and his adventurous approach and choice of collaborators is famous.

Barlaston Mug 1940
page 39

Josiah Wedgwood was born at Burslem in the Potteries in 1730, and worked there from an early age. The firm to which he gave his name remained at the factory built in 1769 for 170 years but with continuous growth, wear and tear and congestion it had become inadequate. In 1940 the firm moved seven miles away to a new factory designed by Keith Murray and C. S. White, at Barlaston.

By April 1940 samples of the commemorative mug designed by Ravilious to mark the occasion had been produced. He wrote to Tom Wedgwood, 'I am very pleased indeed that the yellow and grey version seems the better one. I've no other criticism, the bright orange and blue one isn't really very good – the other is splendidly rich in effect, much richer than I thought it would be. The registration is excellent. I hope they will all be as clear.'[12]

W. B. Honey records that the design was 'a lithograph drawn by Ravilious himself for direct application to the ware'.[13] It was appropriate that the mug should have been produced lithographically at the new Barlaston factory as this process did away with the need for skilled engraving and deft hand colouring; progress that pointed towards the less craftsmanlike and labour-intensive production of the post-war years.

In the absence of a finished drawing, the colour reproduction on p. 39 is taken from 'Eric Ravilious as a Designer' by R. Y. Gooden, *Architectural Review*, December 1946. No pattern number has been traced.

Proposed Designs *c.*1937 & 1941
page 40

From the address inscribed on the drawing, the upper design can be dated later than April 1941, when Eric, Tirzah and the three young Ravilious children moved to Ironbridge Farm, near Shalford in Essex. The registration marks suggest that the pattern was intended for photo-lithographic reproduction, but there is no record of samples being produced.

The lower design only came to light when this book was at the printers. Although stylistically the pattern can be dated *c.*1937, it has had to be included at the end of the chronological sequence.

References

1   Helen Binyon, *Eric Ravilious: Memoir of an Artist*, Lutterworth Press, 1983, p. 57

2   'November 5th 1933', repr. Binyon, op. cit., p. 56

3   Letter to Helen Binyon, 19 August 1936 (courtesy of Anne Ullmann). Quoted, and slightly altered, Binyon, op. cit., pp. 86–8

4   Letter to Helen Binyon, 9 October 1936 (courtesy of Anne Ullmann)

5   Repr. Freda Constable, *The England of Eric Ravilious*, Scolar Press, 1982, plate 30

6   Victor Skellern, *Lectures on Wedgwood*, unpublished MS *c.*1957, Wedgwood Museum, Barlaston

7   Repr. Constable, op. cit., plate 14

8   Quoted Binyon, op. cit., p. 89

9   Letter to Cecilia Lady Sempill, 30 October 1938, Tate Gallery Archive, 8284

10   Pat Gilmour, *Artists at Curwen*, Tate Gallery, 1977, pp. 64–5

11   Letter to Cecilia Lady Sempill, 16 October 1939, Tate Gallery Archive, 8284

12   Letter to Tom Wedgwood, 28 April 1940, Wedgwood Museum, Barlaston

13   W. B. Honey, *Wedgwood Ware*, Faber & Faber, 1948, p. 25